reality check

Q&A Advice on Life, Love, and Relationships

reality check

Q&A Advice on Life, Love, and Relationships

by Alison Bell

Scholastic Inc.
New York Toronto London Auckland Sydney
Mexico City New Delhi Hong Kong

Design: Mark Neston

ISBN 0-439-27218-1

12 11 10 9 8 7 6 5 4 3 2 1   1 2 3 4 5 6/0
Printed in the U.S.A.
First Scholastic printing, April 2001

Hey There!

What's your prob? Stressing about a guy? Worried a friend is mad at you? Need some advice? A reality check? If so, you've come to the right place!

In this book, you'll find a bunch of questions—and answers—to all sorts of issues faced by girls like you. First, you'll find advice on a topic you're likely to think a lot about: guys. Then you can read up on issues about your friends, cliques, school, how to feel your best, and how to deal with your family.

Hopefully, you'll be able to use the answers to these questions to help solve some of the problems in your own life. And even if a problem isn't a carbon copy of yours, you'll at least be able to take away some info that you can apply to your own life. Above all, this book proves that you're not alone. Whatever you're feeling, a lot of other girls are feeling the same way.

Don't believe it? Just keep on reading!

Chapter 1:

First **Feelings:** **Eyes** on **Guys**

You've discovered guys. And they've discovered you. And you've never been so confused in your life.

But don't fret too much. You'll figure it all out. It just takes time and experience. Which is what you're gaining right now.

clueless and guy-less

Q. My friends tell me that all guys care about is what a girl looks like. They tell me that if I wear the right clothes and have the right hairstyle, that guys will fall for me. Well, I'm pretty cute, wear cool clothes, have nice long hair, and am not fat or anything. Why, then, hasn't any guy asked me out or seemed interested in me? Maybe looks aren't that important. Or maybe I'm doing something wrong. I *am* kinda shy around guys. What do you think?

Megan, 13

A. Sure, looks are important in getting a guy to first notice you. But after he does, there's something a lot more important about you than the way you dress or wear your hair. It's that little thing called a personality. Guys are attracted to girls who have good ones—who are nice, funny, friendly, outgoing, and who seem interested in them.

Just think about it. Do you want to hang out with the mega-hunks at your school who have mega-attitudes or the more normal-looking guys with great attitudes? You'd probably take guy-type number two in a heartbeat. Well, guys aren't any different from girls. So stop putting so much effort into your hair and clothes and put more into how you act. Probably, if you just make a slightly bigger effort to be friendly around guys (I know it's hard if you're shy!), you'll find that they'll take an interest in you.

By the way, are you sure you're accurate when you say no one likes you? Maybe you're just not reading the cues right. Is there a guy who says hi to you each day, or asks you how class is going or how you did on a test? Maybe he's not keeling over declaring his love for you, but he *is* showing an interest. So take another look around, and you may discover you have more admirers than you think.

from friend to boyfriend

Q. I've had a good guy friend since fourth grade. I like him a lot, but only as a friend. The other day he told me he

4

A. Wow! What a whammy! But these sorts of things happen. This friend may have fully flipped for you, or he may just be testing the romantic waters. Either way, you need to tell him how you feel (very, very gently).

While things may be awkward between the two of you for a few weeks or even months, over time, you can probably remain friends. He's sure to be disappointed, but with some time, he'll probably get over it. He may even fall for someone else.

too much teasing

Q. There's this guy I know who always teases me. He's not mean about it, but he likes to call me things like "red" (I have red hair). My best friend tells me that he teases me because he likes me. I'm not so sure. The thing is, he's really cute and I *could* like him. But I don't want him to know that if he doesn't feel the same way about me.

Amanda, 12

A. When a guy teases a girl in a nice, friendly way, it generally means that he *does* like her. If this guy wasn't interested in you, he probably wouldn't bother to show you any attention.

However, if you need more "proof" of his feelings, find a time when you can talk to him more seriously. Not mega-seriously about your relationship or anything. Just try to get behind the teasing and have a real conversation. Chat about school, your families, or about something you both like to do. This gives you a chance to get to know each other a little. It also gives you a chance to check out how he acts toward you. If he looks at you while you talk, seems interested in what you're saying, and asks questions about you, these are all signs that he likes you. So don't be afraid to show him your feelings back!

guy wars

Q. My best friend and I like the same guy. This has happened before, and she got him. Well, I don't want that to happen again. However, I heard that this guy likes her better than me, which really bums me out. What can I do to get him to choose me?

Angie, 13

A. Short of brainwashing this dude, you probably can't change the way he feels. And even if you could, would you really want to? It also wouldn't be very fair to your friend. And you'd probably just end up feeling guilty. Instead, set your sights on a guy your best friend *doesn't* like, or better yet, doesn't even *know*. The further apart your romance lives are, the better your friendship will be.

crushing feelings

Q. I have a big crush on this guy at school who is really popular and cute. I know he'll never go for me, but I still like daydreaming about him. On Valentine's Day, I even found an anonymous card to send him. (I ended up chickening out and not sending it.) My best friend says that I'm wasting my time thinking about this guy. But I think it's fun! What's your opinion?

Madelaine, 13

A. Sounds like you've got this crush completely in check. You aren't fooling yourself into thinking this guy's going to fall for you. Instead, you're content to admire him from a distance. When crushes are taken lightly, as you're doing, they're fun and add a little spice to life. It's only when a girl takes one really seriously, and finds herself getting bummed when her crush doesn't return her feelings, that there can be a problem.

One day soon, you'll like a guy who likes you back. Until then, go ahead and have a crush on this guy...or anyone else your heart desires!

missed the boat

Q. This guy liked me for a long time. He was really sweet, but kind of goofy. He wore these ugly glasses and was kinda pudgy. Because of those things, I just couldn't go for him, even though by the end I was considering liking him back. Well, last month, he got a girlfriend. Now he's totally happy with her and hardly talks to me. I feel bummed every time I see them together. What can I do?

Hannah, 14

A. Sad to say, nothing. You let this guy go—and now he's walked into the arms of someone else.

But it's probably for the best. Sounds like you weren't really interested in this guy, even though a part of you wanted to be. The reality is, if he dropped his girlfriend tomorrow and asked you to take her place, you'd probably feel the *exact* same way you used to—that his looks got in your way.

If you can, try to find it in your heart to be happy for him. The quicker you stop mooning over him and turn your attention to another guy, the happier you'll be, too.

Q. I'm really overweight, and am feeling like no boy will ever like me. I've been told I have a great personality and that I'm lots of fun to be with, but no one ever says I'm pretty. I've tried to lose weight in the past, and am on a diet right now. But even if I *do* lose some weight, I will never be skinny like a lot of the other girls. Do you think that a guy will ever look at me?

Julie, 13

A. For sure!! There's no denying that our society is way too wrapped up in the idea that thin is in. But not all guys buy into this. There are a lot of guys out there smart enough not to just judge a girl on how much she weighs. Instead, they look deeper—into what she has to say, her smarts, her talents, and her personality.

It may also be that you're not giving guys a chance to like you. Maybe you're so self-conscious about your looks that you clam up around them and don't show them how funny and interesting you can be. So put your doubts and insecurities on the back burner and let guys get to know the real "great" you.

two-faced guy

Q. This guy at school is really sweet to me when it's just the two of us. He's even told me how much he likes me. But when he's around his buddies, he pretends he doesn't know me. It's like he's a total stranger. I'm so hurt and confused. What's going on?

Tasha, 13

A. Some guys are too embarrassed to show their true feelings about girls around "the guys" because they're worried their friends will make fun of them. So they put on a macho act to impress their buddies.

It's immature. But it happens. And it sounds like it might be happening with this guy.

You have two choices. You can either quit putting so much energy into this guy because you're going to keep getting hurt. Or else talk to him and tell him that his behavior is upsetting you. If he really cares about you, it may motivate him to grow up.

flirt alert

Q. I've been spending a lot of time with this guy at school. We get along great when we're alone, and I feel really special. But when we're around my friends, he flirts with them! He pays them almost as much attention as he does me. What can I do?

Caroline, 14

A. Honesty is the best policy. Tell him that his flirting is really hurting you. Maybe he's a bit of a natural flirt and doesn't realize he's overdoing it. Or maybe he's trying to win over your friends because he thinks it's the best way to win over your heart. Either way, once he learns how you're feeling, hopefully he'll change. But if he doesn't, you may have to question whether this guy is the right one for you.

tough choice

Q. These two boys at school both like me. I don't know what to do! One day I think I like one the best, the next day, I like the other one better. How can I choose between them?

Janie, 14

A. Lucky you! Lots of girls would love to be in your position. And while you're stressing over which guy to like back, maybe you don't have to choose—at least for now. It's okay if you just want to kick back and enjoy the attention—as long as you're not leading either one of them on, which would be hurtful to them.

Over time, and as you get to know them better, you'll probably start to like one more than the other anyway. Just listen to your heart—it will eventually give you the answer you're searching for.

change of heart

Q. Last year, this guy asked me to go to the movies with him, and I said no. I didn't like him then. But this year, he's really changed, and so have I. If he asked me to go to the movies, I'd say yes. Do you think I should tell him how I feel? I hardly ever talk to him anymore, so I don't really know how he's feeling.

Arielle, 13

A. If this guy liked you last year, he might still like you this year. So gather your courage and go talk to him. You don't have to immediately open up with, "Can I take a rain check on that movie?" Instead, first chat about some stuff that's easy to talk about, like school. Then, if everything is going well and he seems happy that you're taking an interest in him, take the plunge and say something like,

"I know that last year you asked me out to the movies, and I said no. Well, my feelings have changed. I'd like to go out if you would." Chances are, he'll take you up on the offer!

just a friend

Q. I've had a crush on this guy, like, forever. We're good friends, and I know he really cares about me, but not that way. How do I know this? Because he's always telling me about other girls he likes. If he only knew how much my heart breaks when he talks to me about other girls. How can I get him to think of me as more than just a friend?

Serita, 12

A. While it definitely takes a lot of courage, the quickest way is to just tell him how you feel. Tell him exactly what you told me—that it hurts you to hear him talk about other girls because you like him as more than just a friend. At first, he'll probably be totally surprised. He may not know what to say or how to react. But after he's had some time to think about what you said, he might start to view you differently, too. Your honesty may allow him to realize deeper feelings he has for you. It's worth a shot—so go for it!

same old story

Q. Every time I like a guy, he doesn't like me. And the guys who like me, well, I don't return their feelings. Am I ever going to find someone I like who likes me back?

Bethany, 13

A. Of course you will. What you're experiencing happens to everybody—both guys and girls. It's tough finding someone you click with. But you will—you just need to spend time around lots of guys and figure out what kind of guy you're meant to be with.

So don't give up. Someday soon, you're going to fall for a guy who has fallen for you. Then all the guys you've suffered over won't matter so much!

locked lips

Q. I've been dating this guy for a while, but we haven't kissed. I think he's going to kiss me soon, and I'm really nervous. I've never kissed a guy before. I don't know how to do it, plus, what if he doesn't like the way I kiss?

Leslie, 13

A. Don't worry! Any boy who likes you will automatically like the way you kiss. As for the mechanics of the lip lock, it's really not hard. All you have to do is put your lips against the guy's and make contact. The rest will happen naturally. Even if you think you don't know what to do, you will when the time comes, despite your nerves—and any nerves your guy has, too!

Chapter 2:

Boyfriends
and Dating

Suddenly, your romance life is moving at warp speed. You're dating, and maybe even have a boyfriend. Or at least a potential boyfriend.

But whichever dude you hook up with, keep one thing in mind. Don't get pressured into a relationship with someone you know deep down *isn't* right. And don't let anyone talk you out of a guy who you know *is* right.

smart decision

Q. There's this really smart, kinda nerdy guy in my Spanish class. Some of the cool kids make fun of him and call him Einstein. When they do, he handles it really well. It seems like nothing gets to him. I admire that, plus, I have to admit, I think he's cute even if he is a bit of a dweeb.

I've heard from a few people that he likes me. I'd like him back too, except that I'm scared that if we got together, everyone would make fun of me. What should I do?

Jennifer, 14

A. Hey, be an Einstein yourself and go for this guy! He sounds really great. As for the cool kids, don't worry about what they say. Maybe they'll laugh or make a comment. But pretty soon, they'll grow tired of it, and move on to teasing the next person on the list.

Also, try not to worry what everybody else will say (even though it's not an easy thing to do). You aren't "everybody." You're yourself. And only you know what's good for you.

age-old problem

Q. I met this guy last weekend at a friend's house. He's a junior in college and really cute. He's 20, but we hit it off so well, you'd never know that I was a lot younger. He called me yesterday and asked if I wanted to meet him at the mall this weekend. I really want to go, but I'd have to lie to my parents because they wouldn't let me go out with a guy that old. Should I meet him?

Alex, 14

A. I think you know the answer. No! For starters, it's definitely uncool lying to your parents. Okay, sometimes you do have to tell a few white ones, but a whopper like this is too big and irresponsible.

Plus, this guy is six years older than you. You have to ask yourself, why does he want to hang around a 14-year-old? (Sure, you're fabulous, but aren't there at least a few fabulous 20-year-old women out there for him?) Some guys like younger girls because they think they can boss them around. They think that younger girls will be less of a challenge than ones their own age. This may be good for them, but not for you.

Call this guy back and tell him that he's too old for you. If he wants to wait until you're 20(!), well, let him. Until then, you'll be hanging with guys your own age.

first date jitters

Q. This cute, nice guy asked me to go to the movies with him and I said yes. My parents are driving us next Saturday afternoon. But now that the date's coming up, I'm feeling really nervous and want to cancel. What should I do?

Alexandria, 13

A. Take the tension out of the situation by turning the movie into a group date. Call the guy and tell him that you'd feel more comfortable inviting along some mutual friends. He'll probably understand and maybe even be relieved himself. Then together you can decide who else to invite.

Group dates are always a good idea because they offer you a way to be comfortable with guys. So next time before you say yes to a solo date, why not make it a group date to begin with?

too close for comfort

> **Q.** My best friend broke up with her boyfriend last month after dating him for a few months. She never talks about him anymore and seems totally over him. Now her ex, "Tom," has asked me to go to the school dance. I think he's really nice and cute, and I want to go. But I'm worried that it will upset her. What do you think I should do?
>
> Chloe, 14

A. From what you've said, it doesn't sound like your best friend and Tom had that serious of a relationship. They only dated a few months, and your friend was the one who ended it. However, before you date her ex, do the right thing and ask her how she would feel if you went to the dance with him. If she's okay with it, then go.

Be warned, however, that your friend may sing another tune if you and Tom get serious. It's one thing for you two to go on one date; she might think it's another if you become a couple.

oh no, he said no

Q. I asked a guy to go to a high school football game with my family because he likes football and my brother is on the team. The guy said no. Just like that. I almost died. The way he responded, it's like he hates me. What should I do? I'm crushed.

Maddie, 14

A. There's no denying that rejection is hard. But everyone goes through it. At least you had the guts to ask a guy out! A lot of girls wouldn't have. You should give yourself a pat on the back for being a courageous member of your gender!

And, as tough as it is to be turned down, don't take it personally. Who knows why this guy said no. Maybe he had to baby-sit his little brother that night. Maybe he already has a girlfriend you don't know about. Maybe he's allergic to talented, wonderful, brilliant, beautiful girls like you. Maybe he was too embarrassed or caught off guard to be gracious.

So don't conclude the guy hates you. On the other hand, don't set yourself up for more possible rejection by asking him out again. Next time, don't be discouraged—just ask out somebody else.

to be or not to be?

> **Q.** I know this wonderful guy from church, and over the last year we've grown really close. Last Sunday at a party, he asked me to be his girlfriend. I was completely shocked. I didn't know what to say, so I didn't say anything. But I know he wants an answer.
>
> I'm not sure what it means to be his girlfriend. I only see him once or twice a week, and we've never even kissed or anything. I also feel too young to get tied down to one guy.
>
> What should I do?
>
> Suzie, 13

A. For starters, feel flattered. This guy has given you a big compliment. Next, follow your heart. It's telling you that you're probably not ready to go steady.

However, it's hard to say exactly what this guy means when he asked you to be his "girlfriend." Maybe he just wants reassurance from you that you like him. Or maybe he wants to start dating. Being a girlfriend or boyfriend is such a loose term, it can mean almost anything. So you might want to ask him exactly what he means. But if he's looking for a one-on-one, just explain, keeping it short and sweet, that while you like him, you're not ready to hang with any one guy exclusively. If he's as great a guy as you say, he'll understand.

double dating

> **Q.** I've been dating two guys at once. For example, last Saturday one guy came over to my house to watch a baseball game. Then that night, I went out for pizza with the other guy. And last week, I met one guy at the high school water polo game (he plays on the team). On another day, I went to watch the other one at his soccer practice. They go to different schools, so they don't know about each other.
>
> It's not like I'm their girlfriend or anything. But I know each one thinks I like him only. My friend says I'm leading them on and being dishonest. I don't really think so. What's your take?
>
> Trish, 14

A. Reality check, girlfriend. You *are* leading them both on. Each guy thinks he's the only one, right?

You could let things keep
going on as they are for a
while, but eventually you
might want to let each one
know about the other. So be hon-
est and tell each one that you're hanging with someone
else as well. You don't have to give all the details, but this
way, at least they'll know the deal.

After a while, you might find that you'll want to
choose one of them for a closer relationship. Juggling
things then might get to be too tricky!

breakup bummer

> Q. My boyfriend that I had all summer long broke up
> with me when school started.
>
> He just suddenly quit talking to me and now has a new
> girlfriend. I want to know two things: Should I ask him
> what happened to us and will I ever get over him?
>
> Maggie, 14

A. Your boyfriend treated you badly, but you may never
know why. Sure, you can ask him. In fact, you *should*.
Because he owes you an explanation. But he may not
be able or willing to give you one. Or at least one that
makes sense to you or satisfies you.

As for Life After the Breakup, please know that you *will* indeed get over this guy, and sooner than you think! Right now you're feeling totally miserable, which is to be expected. But over time, you're going to feel better. And one day, a guy is going to smile at you. And you're going to smile back. And a little light-bulb will go on inside your head that blinks, "There are other guys out there. Cute ones. Ones I could like." And after that day, thinking about your ex won't hurt so much.

Invasion of the
Body Snatchers

Chapter 3:

When you were younger, you probably never gave your looks a second thought, right? You were too busy running around being a kid. But now that you're older, suddenly you scrutinize your body. Your hair. Your skin. Your nose (or at least the bump on it).

Part of the reason is that your body's going through a lot of changes and you're not used to them yet.

Remember this: Someday you'll start to feel more comfy in your skin. It just takes time and a little positive thinking. And liking yourself. And not comparing yourself to super-models. Which brings us to the ability to look at Kate Moss and say, "Hey, I bet she doesn't look that hot without all that makeup, lighting, and airbrushing."

the pain of the gain

Q. I used to be a skinny Minny, but since I started my period, I've gotten fat. I've gained about seven extra pounds, and hate every single one. I have a tummy and I swear my thighs wiggle. And all of my clothes are too tight. Can you recommend a diet that will

A. Hold on there, girl! Newsflash: Gaining seven pounds doesn't make you "fat." Yes, it can be a shock when your body changes. But even with those changes, are you sure your tummy's bulging out and your thighs are wiggling? You're probably being hypercritical of yourself.

And get this: It's normal for girls to gain around 10 pounds or more once they hit puberty (and if you've started your period, you're definitely there). As your body matures, it's supposed to become fuller and curvier. For example, you probably have breasts now. This, in itself, may account for some of the weight gain. Gaining a few pounds at this time in your life doesn't mean something's wrong; it means your body is doing something very right.

If your clothes are too tight, you may have to buy some new ones. And if you go up a size, don't freak. Clothing sizes don't mean much anyway. With one brand, maybe you'll wear an 8; another, a 6. It all depends on the individual clothing manufacturer.

As for diets, don't go on one unless you first see your doctor. She will be able to tell you if it's necessary, and if so, to figure out a safe, sensible one for you to follow.

Despite what you may have heard, there are no "miracle" diets, so avoid any fad ones where you eat only certain types of food, like protein or carbs. The only way to lose weight—and keep it off—is to eat healthy, well-balanced meals, avoid junk food, and get regular exercise—if you even need to lose a pound in the first place! Come to think of it—this is good advice to follow anytime.

flat isn't where it's at

Q. Everyone I know has grown a chest, except for me. I barely even fit into an A cup. My best friend, on the other hand, is a C cup. Everyone is always telling her how great she looks. It's not fair. What should I do?

Samantha, 14

A. Short of having plastic surgery, which is way too drastic of an action, all you can do is accept the size of your breasts—for now, at least. Don't give up on the possibility that they may grow. If you're a late bloomer, your breasts are probably still developing.

But even if they never do go beyond an A cup, there are a few things you can do to look bigger. You can buy a bra with padding. You can also wear shirts with darts or pleats—the gathered material will give the illusion of fuller breasts.

It may help to know that some girls with big chests wish they were smaller. They feel self-conscious about them, and don't like the way their breasts get in the way when they exercise or dance. So life isn't perfect even if you are a C cup. In fact, some of those girls may sometimes look down at their chests and think, "It's not fair!" Plus, look at the positive side: Small-breasted girls look great in halter tops!

too tall

Q. I'm the tallest girl in my eighth grade class and am sick of it. Some of the guys call me "Big Bird" and ask me which basketball team I'm on (I don't even like basketball!). I slump to look shorter, but it doesn't really work. Do you think other kids, especially the boys, are ever going to catch up with me?

Cassidy, 13

A. They sure will, and pretty soon, too. Girls shoot up before guys because guys are slower to mature. But in the next year or so, you'll notice that the boys will start to grow taller themselves. When they do, at least a few are going to tower over you!

In the meantime, however, don't slump! It's a bonus to be tall. Look at all the supermodels—some of them are well over six feet tall, and they're considered some of the most beautiful women on earth! Also, remember that some short people feel like no one takes them seriously.

If you hunch your shoulders, it's a signal to others that you're insecure. That will make people tease you even more because you seem vulnerable. But if you stand tall and proud, you send the message that you're okay with your height—and then others will be, too. Your confidence will act like a force field against teasing, because once kids see that their comments don't get to you, they'll stop making them.

bummed over her big bust

> **Q.** I'm 13 years old and wear a D cup. I'm bigger than my big sister, who is 16, as well as my mom. I feel like some kind of a freak. Plus, it's uncomfortable lugging my breasts around. Another thing is, the guys at school stare at me. Maybe it's my imagination, but I don't think so. I just don't know what to do!
>
> Pammy, 13

A. Hang in there. It's a big adjustment having grown-up breasts at age 13. However, over time you'll get more used to them and one day may even be happy you have them. Some of your physical discomfort may mean that your bra isn't giving you enough support. Make sure you buy one that holds your breasts in tightly and doesn't allow for a lot of wiggling and jiggling.

As for the guys who are staring at you, it all depends on how they're doing it. Guys your age aren't used to seeing girls with breasts, so sometimes their eyeballs bug out without them even knowing or trying to be rude. Shoot them a look back, and they'll probably quickly look the other way.

On the other hand, if a guy is staring at you on purpose and trying to make you nervous and uncomfortable, that's not acceptable. You have two options here. You can talk to him and tell him to stop. If he denies his actions, don't get into a big discussion or anything. Just say stop it again and walk away. He'll get the message. Or, if you don't feel comfortable confronting him (which for sure is hard), or if he doesn't stop, report him to a teacher or another authority figure at school. While you may have doubts 'bout "telling" on him, this guy needs to know that he's out of line.

the calorie club

Q. I hang out with a bunch of girls at school who have started acting really weird. A few months ago, one girl came to school with just some carrots for lunch and started talking about how little she eats each day. Then some of the other girls started bragging about how little *they* ate, saying, "Oh, I just eat a salad for dinner" or "I ate 10 pretzels, and boy did I feel fat afterward."

Now, a lot of the girls are just bringing a yogurt or pretzels for lunch. I'm sick of hearing them talk about food all the time, plus I feel like a pig eating my sandwich and chips. Who has the problem, them or me?

Sarah, 14

A. *They* do. So much so that it sounds like some of them may be well on their way to having an eating disorder. If so, they're not alone. Over five million girls and women suffer from one. There are three types:

❋ **Anorexia**, when girls starve themselves.

❋ **Bulimia**, when girls eat, then purge themselves by vomiting, over-exercising, or using diuretics or laxatives.

❋ **Binge Eating**, when girls eat excessively (like a whole pack of cookies or a quart of ice cream) in a short period of time.

Girls with eating disorders can get really sick. **Anorexics** can lose so much weight that they become dehydrated and malnourished. This can make their blood pressure fall too low and give them heart problems. (Worst case: Sometimes their hearts stop, and they die.) They can feel depressed, worthless, and even want to kill themselves.

Girls with **bulimia** can damage their stomach and their esophagus, the tube leading from the mouth to the stomach, from so much vomiting. Sometimes their teeth decay, too, from all that purging. They're also at risk for having heart problems and for depression.

Binge eaters put themselves at risk for becoming obese. Emotionally, they feel ashamed, guilty, and out of control.

All of these eating disorders share something in common: The girls who have them are obsessed with food and counting calories. While your pals may not have a full-blown eating disorder yet, their eating habits are whacked. It's also not normal to brag about how little you eat or to get caught up in an "I eat less than you so I'm better" mentality. You're smart not to buy into the carrot competition because if you did, you might start freaking about every little thing you eat, too. Then just think how miserable you'd be.

When you're with your pals, bring up other topics to get their minds off food and onto something else. And don't be ashamed of eating healthfully and normally.

And, if the food situation gets too intense, you might try to sit with other friends during lunch.

P.S. If one of your friends appears to have anorexia or another eating disorder (she's losing a lot of weight and/or disappearing after each meal, possibly to throw up), talk to her about it because she needs help. While you can't force her to get help, you can do your best by voicing your concern. Or, tell a parent or other trusted adult about your suspicions, and let that person take the next step.

sticky situation

Q. I have two older brothers, and I've always made fun of how completely gross and stinky they get after playing soccer or baseball. Last week, one day after P.E., I smelled something, something bad. I sniffed under my arm, and I really stunk! But the bigger problem is, I don't just smell after P.E. I smell a little bit all the time. I'm also sweating a lot. The other day I wore this brown dress, and when I raised my hand to answer a question in class, there was a sweat stain on it. The rest of the day, I had to keep my hands at my sides, which was pretty tough considering I had to get through lunch and an art project. What should I do?

Jenna, 12

A. For starters, please know that you're not the only girl on the planet who sweats and stinks. Once puberty kicks in and your sweat glands "turn on," most do, at least a little. They've just learned to wear clothes that don't show sweat stains and they know how to use an antiperspirant.

So don't get down on yourself, get hip to an antiperspirant, which will help stop you from sweating in the first place. You can also try ones that come scented. If it becomes an ongoing concern, avoid bright-colored dresses or shirts. Go for whites or neutrals, and natural fabrics like cotton, which don't leave much of a stain if you turn on the waterworks.

Also, know that just because you sweat a lot now doesn't mean you always will. After your body settles down some, you may find that you perspire less.

oh, how my nose grows

Q. Help! I hate my nose. It's huge. When I smile, it's all I see. Why can't I have a button nose like some other girls? How can I live the rest of my life like this?

Janey, 13

A. By slowly but surely accepting the nose you were born with. And just because you don't like your nose doesn't mean it's not likable. What you focus on as your "worst" feature may actually look very good, even beautiful, to others.

Don't believe it? Ask some of your friends what they "hate" about themselves. You might be amazed at how minuscule their perceived "flaw" seems to you, or that you see it as an asset!

So take another look at your nose. Is it as big and ugly as you think it is? Probably not. Maybe it's not perfect, but whose nose is anyway? Do yourself a favor and try not to focus so much on your nose in the first place. The less of a big deal you make it, the smaller it will seem to you.

Moody **Blues** and Other **Feelings**

Let's face it. Some days are better than others. Some days you click with your friends, ace pop quizzes, and your parents don't nag you. Other days, you fight with your pals, can't concentrate in school, your parents are all over you, and even your dog seems mad at you!

When life's a bummer, you need a little extra support. From others and from yourself. So take a relaxing bath. Read your favorite magazine. Take a walk with a friend. And remember, moods pass. Tomorrow will be a better day.

disappointment diva

Q. When things don't go my way, I get seriously bummed. Like last week I got a C+ on a test instead of the B I thought I was going to get, and I was in a bad mood for two days. The next day a friend of mine ignored me at lunch, and that put me in a terrible mood, too. When I feel down, I take it out on everyone around me. For example, at home, if my little brother is getting on my nerves, even just a little, I really scream at him. I feel like

> I'm getting out of control, and don't know what to do about it. But once a mood sets in, I just can't shake it off!
>
> Lindsey, 14

A. It's normal to feel disappointed when things go wrong. Everybody does. The secret, however, is to not dwell on those feelings for too long.

How to knock them out of your head? Try this: The next time you're bumming over a test or a pal, give yourself 20 minutes to fret about it. Set a timer, and really stew. If you want, write down your feelings in a journal, too.

Once the timer rings, tell yourself it's time to move past feeling bad and to start looking for solutions to your problems. Ask yourself what you can do next time to get a better grade on the test. Or, if you and your friend aren't hitting it off, maybe you need to have a chat to clear the air. After you've come up with a few solutions, write them down. Now you have a plan of action. Simply coming up with one can help you feel better right away because it gives you hope that things can change for the better.

Next, get going. Start studying for the next test or call up your pal. Because you're doing something positive, you'll immediately start feeling better.

As a way of not yelling at your brother (or anyone else who's in the room with you when you're feeling like a total crank), here's a simple but effective solution: Leave the room. If you feel yourself getting irritated, walk away before you have the chance to yell or say anything you'll regret later. Sounds incredibly easy *because it is*!

sudden sadness

Q. I can understand feeling sad when something bad happens, like a friend moves away or your parents split up. But sometimes I feel sad for no reason. One minute I'm completely fine, the next, I feel like I want to cry. Sometimes the feelings go away pretty quickly; other times, they can last all day. If I knew what was wrong, I'd "fix" it, but as far as I know, nothing is wrong. HELP!

Marissa, 13

A. These feelings can be completely normal. Some of your moodiness may be caused by hormones. Or maybe down deep something *is* bothering you, but you just can't pinpoint it yet.

Whatever the cause, it's okay to feel blue now and then, even if you don't know why. You can't feel happy all the time—no one does. Ask any of your friends; they probably feel the same way sometimes.

That said, there's no reason for you to suffer needlessly. One easy way to break a sad (or bad) mood is to exercise. When you do anything aerobic (stuff that gets your heart pounding, such as brisk walking, running, swimming, soccer, or in-line skating), your body releases feel-good chemicals that automatically can improve your attitude. So hit the trail, or the pool, or lace up those skates. You're gonna feel better!

from loser to winner

> **Q.** All of my family and friends are ultra-talented. My best friend plays the piano and is in the school orchestra. My other good friend is a really good soccer player. My older sister is an awesome writer and has her poems published in the high school literary magazine. I don't play an instrument, am a complete klutz in sports, and hate even writing my school assignments. I feel like I'll never be good at anything.
>
> Devin, 12

A. You already are good at something—you just don't know it! So maybe you aren't the next Mia Hamm or are more familiar with the dog Beethoven than the composer. But you have your own unique gifts all the same.

Think about it. Do friends turn to you in times of need and trust you with their secrets? Your talent may be that you're an amazing listener and good friend. Or do you have a special way with animals? Maybe you communicate with your cat like no one else does in the family. Your gift may be working with animals.

Take a look at all you do each and every day, and make a list of what you're good at. Don't leave anything out, for example, that you have the neatest handwriting in your class or can make really cool flower arrangements or that you bake sugar cookies that melt in your mouth. Now, read out loud everything on your list. You'll see just how talented you really are. What's more, as you continue to grow up and experience and learn new stuff, you're sure to discover other things (that you don't even know about yet) that you're good at!

friend in need

Q. I've had the same best friend for eight years. Lately she's super-sensitive about everything and always seems to be bummed out. I don't think I've seen her

A. Sounds like your pal is depressed. While it's normal to feel down sometimes, there's a difference between feeling bummed over something for a day or two and being depressed.

Some symptoms of depression are:

❋ feeling bad for weeks at a time

❋ losing your appetite or eating too much

❋ not being able to concentrate at school

❋ not being interested in things you normally are

❋ sleeping a lot or not sleeping at night

❋ withdrawing from friends and family

People who are depressed need help. Talk to your friend and tell her your concerns. Encourage her to talk to her parents or other adults she trusts because these are the people who are in a position to help her. If your friend won't listen to you, and you're still worried after talking to her, tell an adult about the situation and ask him or her to take over from there.

to talk or not?

Q. When I get down, sometimes I talk about it with my friends. Some of them are really sympathetic; some act like they couldn't care less. I'm confused. What should I do, and why are some of my buds acting this way?

Chelsea, 12

A. Tell the ones who are unsympathetic how you're feeling. Maybe they don't realize they're coming across as uncaring. Or maybe they're so wrapped up in their own problems that they aren't able to be good listeners right now.

But also it could be that you're telling them *too* much. Most friends are happy to lend a listening ear to a few probs. But if you're always dumping a big wad of woes on friends, they may feel overwhelmed and want to run for cover. In defense, your buds may act uninterested. This may be their way of saying, "Enough, please!"

It also depends on *who* you're telling. Good friends are usually there to listen to you when you're down (as long as you're not over-using them). Casual friends, on the other hand, may not be that connected to you and therefore not as interested. So save the nitty-gritty for your best pals. And just as important, be there for *them* when they need to talk!

one busy gal

Q. I'm only in seventh grade, but already I feel super-stressed. I play soccer, sing in the school choir, am in math tutoring, and take violin lessons. Every afternoon, all I do is run around from activity to activity. Then, sometimes I have to sit through my sister's music lessons or whatever she has going on. By the time I get to bed, I feel tired, plus behind. There's never enough time to practice my violin or do my extra math homework on top of everything else. I feel so burned out. Can you give me some advice?

Samantha, 13

A. You've got a right to be stressed. You, like a lot of teens, are over-scheduled. You've got way too much to do and not enough time to do it in. So the time has come to cut some activities from your busy day—as long as your folks say okay.

Look at your weekly calendar and find at least one thing to drop. Maybe, for example, you're no longer interested in playing the violin and just have been keeping up with the lessons out of habit. Next, ask your folks if you can take a break from the activity for a month. If, at the end of the month, you miss it, you can decide to go back. But if you don't miss it, suggest that you'd like to drop it permanently, or at least for another few months and see how you feel then.

Once you adjust your schedule, you'll automatically feel less stressed. As for being dragged around to your sis's activities, make the best of it by bringing along any work you can do on the road. That way when you get back home, you'll have some time to just chill.

Chapter 5

Friendship Fixes

Friendships are super-important. Friends make things better when you're feeling down, and they can make your day with some happy news. But every friendship has its bumps along the way. You just need to learn how to handle 'em.

the big green monster

Q. This is really hard to admit, but I'm jealous of my best friend. She's super-cute, is a great student, and everyone loves her. I love her, too, but sometimes I get sick of hearing how wonderful she is. When I feel this way, I don't even want to be around her. And sometimes I end up snapping at her. What can I do? It's just so hard being friends with Miss Perfect!

Jen, 12

A. Give yourself some credit for having the courage to admit your feelings. Lots of girls are jealous of their friends but don't have the guts to fess up! Plus, now that your jealousy is out, you can meet it—and beat it—head on.

One way to do this is to stop focusing so much on your pal and more on yourself. Find something you like to do and feel good about, whether it's playing the oboe, joining the softball team, or designing your own Web page. The more success you have in your own activities, the better you'll feel about yourself—and the more you'll start feeling good about sharing your friend's successes!

P.S. By the way, your friend isn't perfect, you know. If you asked her what she needed to improve, she'd probably give you a big, long list. She may even say that she's jealous of *you* sometimes. If so, it'd be good for you to have her tell you how!

seeing double

Q. Help! I have this friend who keeps copying me. If I wear something, she wears practically the same outfit the next day. If I wear my hair in braids, she puts hers in braids, too. If I call something "radical," so does she. I'm starting to feel like the Doublemint twins! What can I do to get her to stop?

Diana, 13

A. Gee, you two probably look real cute in your matching outfits—just kidding! Sounds like your pal is insecure. She's scared no one will like the real her. So she figures she'll play it safe and be someone else—you! (Which is a *kind* of flattery, if you think about it.)

The solution? Find something unique about her to compliment. Maybe it's her cool headband or funky shoes or the cute way she says, "Gee whiz." (Hint: Find something you really *do* like; if you fake your admiration, you'll be setting her up for failure because she'll get negative feedback from others for being herself.) The more positive reaction your friend gets for being uniquely herself, the less she'll feel the need to copy you, and pretty soon, your problem should be solved.

fickle friend

Q. I have a good friend who lives down the street. We hang out together a lot after school and on the weekends. At school, however, it's a different story. She hardly ever talks to me and sometimes cuts me down in front of her friends.

Two questions: Do you think she's acting this way because I'm uncool, and is she a true friend?

Morgan, 13

A. You are totally *not* uncool! What *is* uncool is being two-faced, like this girl is being. Most likely, she's insecure. She may be so worried about fitting in at school that she sacrifices her "home" friends for the sake of being popular in class. But if she really felt good about herself, she'd have the confidence to openly like anyone she wants—all the time.

As for your second question, sorry to say, this "friend" is no friend. She's happy to make nice when no one else is around. But add a few other people, and she ditches you. A friend is nice to you *all* the time, no matter who or where you are.

Until this girl drops her "I'll only speak to you in the neighborhood" act, you might want to drop *her*—especially if being friends with her under these conditions is too painful for you. You deserve better! This doesn't mean you have to be rude to her or have a big confrontation. Just quit hanging around with her as much after school.

'bye, 'bye, best friend

Q. HELP! My very best friend on earth is moving to California. I live in Arizona, which is not that far away, but it might as well be China! How am I going to survive without her? And what can I do to make sure we still stay friends? We've been buds since kindergarten and I don't want to lose her.

Sophia, 12

A. It's tough when your BF moves away, but you can stay in close touch, especially with e-mail. (If you have Internet access but don't already have an e-mail address, ask your folks if they'll create one for you right away. Have your friend do the same.) And you can chat by Instant Messager, too, if you both have AOL's software, which you can download for free at their site. And there's always the phone. And visits.

As for surviving without your numero uno pal, you can—and you will. You'll just have to lean a little harder on your other friends. And try to make a few new ones. With a little effort, you'll find that it's not as hard as it seems.

aching to be dear abby

Q. I have a good friend who is always asking for my advice, but then never takes it. For example, she fights a lot with her mom because she sneaks out of the house wearing her mom's clothes without permission. So I told her, stop wearing your mom's stuff without asking. My friend nodded her head like she agreed, but today, she showed up at school in her mom's new sweater. So of course, if her mom finds out, they are going to get into another big fight. What can I do to get my friend to take my advice?

Blair, 13

A. Nada. And it has nothing to do with the advice you're giving, which sounds right on. It sounds like your friend, even though she may ask, doesn't really want your opinion. She just wants someone to listen to her—to be her sounding board. The problem is, you want her to get her act together and solve her issues.

Quit wasting your time playing Dear Abby. And if you find it too frustrating being around this friend, start spending more time with other friends and less time with her.

tall tales

Q. One of my friends is the biggest exaggerator. For example, if we have to wait for ten minutes in a line to see a movie, she'll tell people that we stood in line for an hour. Or when she had the flu and had a 100-degree fever, she told everyone that her fever was 103. I could go on and on listing all the times she's stretched the truth. It doesn't hurt anyone, but it drives me crazy! Should I call her on it?

Nan, 14

A. It depends. If something she says is so far out there you can't stand it, feel free to pipe up if it will make you feel better. But be aware that this probably won't do much because the exaggerations are going to just keep on flowing.

Your best bet may be to accept your pal for who she is. Some people just enjoy exaggerating. And like you said, it's not like she's hurting anyone.

Besides, don't think you're the only one who knows she exaggerates. Others probably know, too!

feuding friends

Q. Lately it seems like all my best friend and I do is fight. Over stupid, stupid things. Like yesterday, for example, when we fought about where to eat lunch. Or the day before, when we argued about whose sweater was warmer. Once we even got into a fight about how stupid our fights are. I'm so sick of it, but I don't know what to do.

Megan, 12

A. The simple solution? Take a breather from each other. You two may be suffering from too much togetherness. If you hang with one person too much, sometimes you can get sick of each other and tempers can flare.

You don't have to "break up" or anything. Just take a time-out from each other and instead do a few things with other friends. Eat lunch with another friend for a change. Or invite someone else over on Saturday night. By cutting down on the time you spend together, you'll cut down on the fighting. And if you stop spending so much time together, you'll probably find that you value the times you *do* spend together even more!

is it just my imagination or what?

Q. For some reason, my best friend's parents don't like me. I don't know what I've done to them, but I wish they'd stop being so cold. They hardly ever talk to me. And when they do, they aren't very friendly. The weird thing is, I asked my friend why her parents hate me and she said they like me. But she must be lying. If they liked me, wouldn't they be nicer to me?

Suzanna, 12

A. Not necessarily. Maybe this is just how her parents are. Watch how they act around other people. Do they treat them differently or the same as you? If it's the same, then you know not to take their behavior personally.

However, even if your friends' parents are frosty, you might be able to get them to warm up. How? By showing off your very best manners. Address them respectfully. Ask them how they are. Smile at them. Take an interest in whatever home project they're working on. Maybe you'll never be best buddies with your best pal's parents, but at least you can try to thaw out the relations a little.

fading friendship

Q. My best friend and I have been pals forever. But lately, she's acting distant. When I call her, she has nothing to say. When we do stuff together, she never asks how I am. And at lunch, she's started sitting with another group of girls. I feel like she's "outgrown" me, but I'm not sure. This has never happened before, and I'm so confused!

Jen, 12

A. Talk to your friend. Find a time when you can be alone with her and ask her straight out why she's acting differently. After all, you've been best buds this long, so you deserve to know what's going on with her. Maybe she'll reassure you that she's still your best pal, and give a good explanation for her behavior. If she then starts making an effort toward you again, you'll know the friendship is back on track.

However, if she reassures you that nothing's changed, but doesn't change the way she acts, or if she tells you flat out that it's time to go your separate ways, you've got no choice but to accept the fact that she's moving on.

As hard as it is, sometimes friendships don't last. People change. And when they do, they don't always have as much in common with their old pals anymore.

Maybe the friendship will blossom again, maybe not. But in the meantime, take this opportunity to start spending more time with some of your other friends. While losing a friend hurts, it will hurt less if you surround yourself with other friends who care about you.

the secret's out

Q. I can't believe it. I told a secret to a good friend and let her know several times that it was confidential. Well,

A. First of all, give yourself some time to cool down. You won't help the situation if you get all hot-headed around your friend.

Once you've settled down, talk to her. Tell her what you know and ask her to explain. If your friend did spill the beans, there's no denying that. However, your feelings may change when you learn how—and why—she did. Maybe she didn't mean to. Maybe the secret slipped out and she feels completely miserable and would do anything to change it. If this is the case, you'll probably feel like forgiving her.

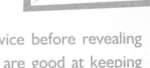

In the future, however, think twice before revealing anything else to her. Some girls are good at keeping secrets; others just can't help blabbing.

possessive pal

Q. My best friend, "Melissa," gets jealous when I talk to other people. Last week, for example, I started to sit with someone else at lunch when Melissa practically

A. Your friend Melissa is holding on way too tight. It's not fair to you. The first thing to do is to stop giving in to her threats. She thinks that she can pressure you into being her one and only pal, and, because you give in to her, her plan is working! As you no doubt already know, friendship isn't about hanging out together exclusively 24/7. True friends—people who really care about you—give you the space to do your own thing and make other friends.

Why not have a heart-to-heart with Melissa? Explain to her that while you care about her, you also want to spend time with other friends. Reassure her that liking others won't take away from how much you like her. Then encourage her to branch out and make some new friends of her own.

Even if she pouts, don't back down. And if she says something like, "If you make new friends, I won't be your friend," call her bluff and say okay. Within a short while she'll probably regret her words and ask you to be her friend again. It's fine to take her back—as long as you add, "But we still need to spend time with other friends."

Hopefully Melissa will change. If not, however, you may need to end the friendship, at least for now. While you'll miss her, you won't miss the way she didn't let you have other friends.

flirty friend

Q. This friend of mine is driving me bonkers. All she does is talk about guys. I like to talk about them too, but not 24/7! Plus, she completely embarrasses herself around them. She turns into such a mega-flirt that all she does is giggle. Should I tell her how annoying she's being?

Amelia, 12

A. No. If you pick on her behavior around guys, she's bound to feel hurt. Plus, are you sure she's being that embarrassing? Maybe the guys like her giggles!

However, it is okay to tell her that you'd like to talk about something besides guys. School. Sports. The upcoming dance. Whatever. As long as it's not about guys. You could do this casually by teasing her. For example, the next time she launches into her twentieth guy story, you could give a loud groan and say,

"Not guys again!!!!" Or you could have a gentle but serious chat with her. Say something like, "Gee, it seems like you love to talk about guys. I do, too, but I also like to talk about other things. Remember all the great discussions we used to have? I miss them."

This may not work, but at least it's worth a shot. And who knows? Maybe soon you'll be so bitten by the boy bug, too, you'll think that everything she has to say is absolutely fascinating!

three's a crowd

Q. I've had these two best friends forever. But lately, they've been telling secrets in front of me. They also went to the movies without me last Saturday. I'm feeling hurt and left out, and am wondering if they want to break up our threesome. What do you think?

Tiffanie, 13

A. Their behavior doesn't mean the threesome is over. Three can be a tough number for friends, because it's common for two girls in the trio to temporarily bond together more. But in a while, usually everyone is clicking together again.

Talk to the twosome and tell them how you're feeling. If they really care about you and your feelings—and hopefully they do—they'll start including you more in their conversations and get-togethers.

Even if they turn back into model friends, however, now's a good time to branch out so you won't be so dependent on this duo in case this happens again. So invite that new girl down the street over or get active in a club that has some other really cool members. Three can be a magic number for friends, but so can four, five, or six!

the silent treatment

Q. I got in a fight with a good friend of mine a week ago and we're still not talking to each other. The thing is, I think she started it. But I heard from another friend that she thinks *I* started it. I really care about her and miss her, but I don't want to be the first to say I'm sorry when it wasn't really my fault. How can I get her to apologize?

Jeannie, 14

A. It's only human that you want her to apologize first. However, you're missing a big point: It's not important who started the fight. When two people fight, they almost always think the other person started it. What's important is that somebody ends it so you two can get back to being friends.

Swallow your pride—it's hard for sure, but necessary—and apologize. Like today. Without thinking twice again about who is really to blame. And without mentioning it when you apologize. You'll be glad you did. And so will your friend. And guess what? She'll probably follow your lead and apologize, too!

hello, old friend?

Q. I had a good friend all throughout elementary school. But last year in seventh grade, she dropped me and hooked up with this other "faster" crowd. Now my friend is coming back to me. She's talking to me in the halls, and has called me a few times. Yesterday at lunch, she walked up to me and my friends and asked if she could eat with us. I didn't know what to say, but ended up saying "yes." I think it's great that my friend is out of that bad crowd. But I'm not sure I should take her back as a friend. What if she drops me all over again? I really cared about her and could again. What should I do?

Mallory, 14

A. Give your friend a second chance. It sounds like she made a mistake and knows it. Because she's been such a good friend, it's worth taking the risk. Before you fall back into the friendship, however, talk to her about your fears. Tell her that while you've missed her and want to reconnect, you're scared that history will repeat itself. This will give both of you a chance to clear the air. It may take you a while to totally trust her again, but that's okay. After all, you're taking a chance. Hopefully as the weeks and months go by, she'll prove her loyalty to you and you can start kicking back and feeling more relaxed around her.

boyfriend blues

Q. My best friend got a boyfriend over the summer, and now she hardly has any time for me. All she talks about is "Matthew this and Matthew that." And any time I ask her to do anything, she's already booked up with Matthew. She hardly calls me anymore, and I'm like feeling totally abandoned. What should I do?

Maggie, 14

A. Hang in there. Sometimes when a girl first starts dating a guy, she gets so wrapped up in him that she drops everything—and everyone. This is a bummer for her friends, but it happens. Usually, however, once the novelty of the relationship wears off, most friends bounce back to their former selves because they realize that they need their girl pals as much as they want their boyfriend.

In the meantime, you might want to talk to your friend and tell her how you're feeling. This might be a wake-up call for her to start acting like a friend again. But keep in mind that even if she becomes more accessible, things will probably never go back to the way they were. Her boyfriend is bound to continue taking up some of her time—time she used to spend with you. So take this opportunity to get to know some other girls—girls who aren't so wrapped up in a guy!

Chapter 6

Fitting In

Y ou're in. You're out. You're popular. You feel like a loser.

Sometimes it's hard to know exactly where you stand on the social scale.

But as intense as the scene gets, don't forget to stay true to yourself. And your friends. Because that's what really matters.

all alone

> **Q.** I hate my school. It's filled with a bunch of snobs. Everyone hangs around in tight little cliques. You couldn't break into one with a bulldozer. I do have one friend, but we don't even like each other that much. We just hang out with each other because there's no one else. What can I do to fit in more?
>
> Lauren, 13

A. It's tough feeling so lonely. And it's tough being surrounded by all those cliques. But things will get better. Here's how: Get involved. Join the soccer team, a dance class, or the school yearbook committee. It doesn't matter what you do, as long as you do something that you enjoy. You've probably heard this all before, but it really works!

This extracurricular stuff will give you a chance to know people away from their little cliques. And as you do get to know them, some will become friends. They'll in turn introduce you to *their* friends. And pretty soon, you'll be in the social loop. So give yourself a little time. Make a little effort. And have a little faith. You'll find at least one or two friends. Promise. And who knows—you might find that you've started a clique of your own!

popularity pointers

Q. My friend and I disagree big time! She thinks that the most popular people in our school got that way because they're nice and friendly. I say they got that way by being mean and fake. Of course, my friend is more popular than me, so she has a higher opinion of popular people than I do. Who do you think is right?

Camille, 13

A. You both have a point. To be popular, you generally have to be friendly and outgoing or no one will like you in the first place. Problem is, some kids, once they become well liked, abuse their popularity by acting all superior to anyone lower down on the food chain.

The best way to be—and stay—popular is, for starters, to be yourself. Ever noticed how the popular kids aren't followers, they're leaders? They wear a cool pair of pants, and by the next week, everyone else is running out to buy a pair. They aren't afraid to be a little different, and people respect that.

Also, be open and friendly. Smile at people, say hi, and be interested in what they have to say. And if you *do* find yourself on top of the popularity mountain, don't change. Don't change a bit.

blow out the candles

Q. I hang out with a crowd of about six girls. I really like everyone except for this one girl. She's new to the group and acts kinda goofy. I've tried talking to her, but I don't have much to say to her. I'm not sure she likes me very much, either.

I have two questions: Do I have to be nice to her when I see her even if I don't like her? Also, I'm having a party in a few weeks for my thirteenth birthday. Do I have to invite her? I really don't want her there.

Olivia, 12

A. First question first. Yes, you should be nice to her. It would hurt her feelings if you gave everyone else a big cheery "Good morning," then looked the other way when you got to her. (Plus, it doesn't make you look good to your other friends if you're mean to someone else.) Think about how you would feel if she treated you this way. You'd be bummed. So show this girl the same respect that you'd want her—or anyone—to show you. However, this doesn't mean this girl has to become your best pal. If you two don't click, fine; not everyone in a clique will be bosom buddies. But even so, don't dis her!

As for inviting her to your party, yup, ya gotta invite her! Why? Because if you don't, it will hurt her feelings. If you ask everyone except her, she'll feel left out. (And if you think you can keep the party a secret from her, you're wrong. She'll find out.) If she decides not to come, that's her choice. But the important thing is, you gave her a choice.

wrecked by a rumor

Q. I got into an argument with a girl at school and she started a rumor about me. Well, the rumor had a lit-

A. Control the damage by marching up to the biggest gossip in school and telling her your side of the story. She'll spread the word, and this will give people a second version to think about.

After that, don't talk about the rumor anymore. The quicker you drop the subject, the quicker others will, too. Soon there will be a new hot rumor to take its place and everyone will forget about it anyway.

courted by the in crowd

Q. I've had the same best friend for years. I love her and can trust her with anything.

But now I'm getting into this whole other crowd of kids at school. They're really popular, and I can't believe they want me to hang around them, but they do. The problem is, they've made it clear that they don't want to include my best friend in their crowd. In fact, one of the girls called her a "loser."

A. Probably not. And maybe you don't want to hear this, but the first person you need to think about is your best friend. Would it be fair to drop someone who has been true blue to you for years for a crowd of girls you just hooked up with? A crowd, by the way, that sounds pretty nasty if they're playing favorites, breaking up friends, and labeling your BF a loser.

It's understandable that you're excited to be part of this cool crowd. It always feels good to be accepted by others you think are out of your reach. Maybe a part of you has been wanting to spread your wings and meet new people anyway. However, if the price you have to pay is rejecting your best friend, that's a hefty price tag!

Even if you try to juggle your friend and the crowd, what's going to happen, when, for example, you're walking with the group in the hall and the girls shoot you dirty looks when you talk to your friend? Or when you're eating lunch with the group and you don't feel like you can invite your friend over? Time and again, you're going to be put in the position of choosing between your friend and the crowd, and you're going to get sick of it. (So will your friend—big time.) You say you want to keep your best friend, but this way, eventually, you'll lose her.

So think carefully about what you're about to do. Because it's a big choice. And it's one only *you* can make.

breaking out of her shell

> **Q.** I'm pretty and smart and fit in pretty well wherever I go. I think I could have a lot of friends, but I have a huge problem. I'm super-shy. When I'm around people I don't know very well, I find it hard to say very much. Sometimes guys tease me about being so quiet, and it really hurts! What can I do to stop being so shy?
>
> Mary Rose, 12

A. Hey, quiet people are just fine, thank you. After all, if everyone walked around being a loudmouth, we'd all have huge headaches. Pep talk aside, it can be hard when you don't know what to say. So, here's the scoop: Start by asking a question. Asking questions is a great way to open a conversation because it puts the burden on the other person to do most of the talking. Plus, as you've probably already noticed, most people love to blab (and blab and blab) about themselves.

Your questions don't have to be brilliant or clever. Anything, ranging from, "Where did you get that pretty skirt?" to "How did you do on the bio exam?" is perfectly fine. Once the person answers your question, ask a follow-up one, such as, "What was the toughest part of the test for you?" Before you know it, the other person will be asking you some questions, you'll be answering, and you'll find yourself in the middle of—surprise!—a conversation.

bully for you

Q. There's this crowd of guys at school who are complete bullies. They yell mean things at almost anyone who walks by. They make girls cry all the time. Last week they picked on me, and I laid into them. I told them they were a bunch of jerks. But then they went after me even more and I ended up crying, too. Now I'm scared to ever walk by them again. What should I do?

Magda, 13

A. Good for you for sticking up for yourself! And while you think it didn't work, maybe actually it did. Next time, maybe these bullies won't pick on you. Bullies tend to victimize those who don't fight back because they like easy targets.

However, this isn't to say you should try to get in a shouting match with them again. When it's one against a crowd, that one person is almost always gonna lose.

Bullies are a big problem at every school, and it's never easy dealing with them. You could report them to the principal, but the principal probably already knows they're problems. Guys like this always seem to find a way to continue their act even if they're reprimanded.

Your best bet is to walk with a few friends whenever you have to pass these guys because they're less likely to pick on you if you're not alone. So buddy up—the more the merrier.

Sibling
Rivalry

Your brother is driving you up a wall. Or maybe it's your sister. And you're thinking, "Why couldn't I have been an only child?"

But even when you feel like blasting your siblings into outer space, you still love them. And they love you.

So try to be a bit more caring around them, a little more patient. Who knows? Maybe your siblings will (someday) return the favor. And life will be a little easier.

in big sister's shadow

Q. Everyone is always comparing me to my sister, who is two years older than me. For example, when I tried out for the swim team, the coach got really disappointed because I didn't swim as fast as my sib. Or when I tried out for the school play, all the drama teacher could talk about was how great my sister was in *Godspell* last year. I try to be as good as her in everything, but I'm just not. How can I make people stop comparing her to me?

Katherine, 12

A. By not trying to be a carbon copy of your big sis and instead being yourself. The harder you try to be like her, the worse you'll feel because you're not giving your own talents a shot!

For example, maybe you aren't as hot a swimmer or actress as your sister. So what? If you like to swim or act, stay the course. If not, put your energies toward something you enjoy more, whether it's ballet, drawing, or running. Once you start pursuing interests different from your sister's, people will stop comparing the two of you. And so, finally, will you!

battle with the brother

Q. My big brother is wrecking my life because he's always teasing me. Whenever he sees me talking to a guy at school, he starts calling the guy my "boyfriend." Or if I drop something in the kitchen, he'll call me a klutz-o-matic. I get really mad and tell him to stop, but he won't. And my parents don't do anything about it. Can you help?

Nicole, 13

A. Luckily for you, there's a secret weapon you can use against your brother. It's called silence.

The next time he opens his big mouth to tease you, act like you couldn't care less. Don't protest or put

up any kind of a fuss. Instead, play mute.

People who tease others like to get a response. But if they don't get one, they're likely to lose interest and quit the ribbing.

So the next time your brother calls you a klutz-o-matic, ignore the comment. Even if he repeats it a few times, don't say anything. The next time, you'll see, he'll tease you a little less. The next, even less. Then one blessed day you'll wake up and find yourself in a tease-free household. (Well, maybe not completely.) But it should work pretty well. Try it.

little sister blues

Q. My little sister is six years old. Whenever my friends are over she barges into my room and wants to hang out with us. We don't want to be with her, but I can't get her to stay away. My mom doesn't think this is a big problem, but it is to me. What can I do?

Terri, 13

A. The easiest solution would be for your mom to simply tell your sister to respect your privacy. But since it doesn't sound like that's going to happen any time soon, you'll have to get creative.

One idea is to ask your mom to arrange a play date for your sister when you have friends over. That way she'll have her own pal to keep her busy and occupied.

Or, try giving your little sister some task that will make her feel involved, but will put some distance between her and you and your friends. For example, if you and your buds are studying bio, ask her to gather some leaves for you. This may not take up too much time, but at least it gives you a little break.

If all else fails, go to a friend's house instead. Unless she's got a pesky little sister, too, that is!

battle of the bedroom

Q. My eleven-year-old sister and I share a room. We're always getting into huge fights about stuff, like how messy her half of the room is or who gets the room alone or how one of us can't study because the other one is listening to the CD player. It's so bad I'm considering living in the garage—if only my parents would let me! We're going to have to share this room for another five years at least, and I just don't know how we're going to survive.

Jessica, 13

A. Call a truce by sitting down with your sister and coming up with some bedroom rules. Start the meeting by going over all the stuff you fight about. Then come up with some rules you can both live with. For example, you might agree to ban all music when one is studying or make sure whoever's listening to music uses headphones. Or to let each other have the room alone for an hour each day. Or to pick up your room each morning.

Write down the rules. Then all that's left is to post the rules in your room and try to live by them. Ask your parents if they'll help you enforce them. While these guidelines probably can't stop all of your skirmishes, at least they'll stop a total war from breaking out.

sneaky sister?

Q. Every time I bring home a friend from school, she gets to know my older sister and starts liking her better than me. It's true. My friends always seem to want to talk to her more than me. Sometimes I think they just come over to see her. What can I do—because I'm sick of her stealing my friends!

Emily, 13

A. Hate to question your reality, but are you *sure* your friends like your sister better than you? Maybe they *do* like her. But not necessarily better than you. And are you sure your sister's trying to steal them from you? Maybe she's just having fun and happy that she gets along with your pals. So don't get all paranoid if you don't have to.

That said, it can be a drag sharing your friends with your sister. So do two things. One, talk to your sib. Ask her nicely if she could give you and your friends some space when they come over. Maybe she could have her own friends over or go to somebody else's house. Go ahead and tell her that you're jealous— maybe it will help her to understand and back off a little.

Two, ask your friends over when you know your sister won't be there. This way you can relax with your best buddies instead of feeling like you have to compete for their attention.

oh, brother!

Q. My brother is a year older than me. You'd think that my own brother would be nice to me at school, but he's not. In fact, if I walk up to him and try to talk to him, he ignores me. Once one of his friends said something mean about me, and he even laughed.

My brother and I used to be really close, but lately he started hanging with the cool crowd while I'm still plain old me. I always thought he'd look after me, but now he's doing the opposite. Help!

Jasmine, 13

A. Your brother needs a wake-up call. A major one. This is no way to treat a sister! This is no way to treat anyone!

Maybe he's somehow clueless to how cruel he's being. He's so caught up in fitting in that he's not even thinking about you—or anyone—but himself. Or maybe he knows. Inside he's sorry, but he's just too desperate to be cool. Either way, you've got to talk to him. Tell him how much he's hurting you. Unless he's morphed into a completely unfeeling human being, he's going to feel bad about his behavior and try to change.

Don't expect miracles overnight, however. You may have to endure a few more of his snubs—with you telling him again how much it hurts—before he kicks the mean act. Hopefully, however, the message will eventually sink in, and he'll start acting more like the brother he used to be.

cut the competition

Q. My sister and I are 18 months apart. She is super-competitive about everything. Like who gets to eat the first bowl of cereal, who gets to watch which TV show, and even who gets to push the buttons on the elevators. She's always butting ahead of me and making everything a competition. I'm totally sick of it. Any suggestions?

Nicola, 12

A. The next time your sister tries to "win" a privilege, beat her to the punch and give in to her. For example, if there's only one chocolate chip cookie left in the jar and you know she's going to fight for it, say, "Why don't you have the last cookie?" Or, before you even turn on the TV suggest, "Let's watch what you want today." This doesn't mean you have to give in to her for the rest of your life. But if you let her have her way, chances are, she'll start being more gracious herself. She may back off and let you win a few times. That way you'll both be winners!

Welcome to My Parents

In your eyes, your parents used to be the greatest two people on earth. But then you grew up. And now you can't help but notice that they've got some quirks. Or even flaws. Enough to make you want to go live with someone else's family every now and then!

Okay, so the parental units aren't perfect, but who is? They're human. Just like you. So cut them some slack. And if something's bugging you, talk to them about it. Maybe they won't see an issue the way you see it. But maybe they will. But if you don't talk to them about it, things will never have the chance to change.

burned by bun-bun

Q. My dad is driving me crazy! The other day I had a bunch of friends over, girls and guys, and he launched into some stories about how adorable I was when I was little. He went on and on about what a chubby baby I was and how I used to love my stuffed rabbit, Bun-Bun. He even told them that I slept with Bun-Bun until I was eight years old! I was so mortified I wanted to

A. Parents. Did you ever think they'd grow up and be so difficult? Especially when they start heading down memory lane with a totally embarrassing story for each year of your entire life! However, it may help you to know that your dad didn't mean to make you want to melt into the carpet. He thinks of you as his little girl and figures you—and your friends—will think his stories about you are as delightful as he finds them.

The answer, then, is to enlighten him. Gently remind him that adolescence is a very sensitive time and that these stories, while innocent enough, truly embarrass you. So even though you and he shared Bun-Bun, as well as many other wonderful memories, *could he please not share them with your pals*?

Since your dad no doubt didn't mean to upset you in the first place, he'll probably stop telling those stories. And if he ever forgets and starts to launch into one, just clear your throat and sweetly say, "Dad, remember? We're not talking about that." Even the most oblivious dad will get the hint!

Q. I love my little sister and brother, but I hate watching them all the time. Problem is, whenever my mom has to run to the store or goes out with my dad, they always make me baby-sit. And they never pay me. My parents think it's easy because my brother and sister are good when they're home. But when I'm alone with them, they turn into complete brats. Plus, it's hard to plan because I never know when my parents are going to ask me to watch them. HELP! What should I do?

Ashley, 14

A. Doesn't seem like your parents are being fair. Sounds like they're putting too much responsibility on you and that it's fair of you to suggest that you be paid to baby-sit. The truth is, however, that you may not be able to change the situation. Even when you think your parents are wrong, they still have the final say because they're in charge. But this doesn't mean you can't try to change things by talking to them.

Choose a time when they're relaxed and have a good chunk of time to spend with you undistracted, like maybe right after dinner. Make sure your brother and sister are in another room so you can have some privacy. Once you have your parents' attention, explain to them what you told me.

Next, ask your parents if they would consider doing any or all of the following three things: 1) hire a baby-sitter sometimes so the burden won't always fall on you; 2) give you at least a few days' notice if you're needed to sit so you can arrange your schedule accordingly; and 3) pay you.

Hopefully your parents will agree to some or all of your suggestions. If they don't, however, why not see if you can invite a friend over when you baby-sit so at least you'll have some company?

overprotective parents

Q. My parents are way too protective. They won't let me stay out late at night or let me go alone after school to a friend's home if her parents aren't there. And wherever I go, they want me to check in all the time. All of my friends have a lot more freedom. They don't have half the hassles I have. What can I do to get my parents off my back?

Jill, 14

A. Make them stop loving you so much! Just kidding, 'cuz it's not going to happen. Since that's the reason they put restrictions on you. Not because they're power-hungry or angry or want to make your life miserable. They care about your safety and well-being. That's what good parents do.

From what you've said, your parents aren't really being unreasonable, even if it sounds as though they are. For example, it often *is* a bad idea to hang out at someone's house when her parents aren't there. Things could happen. Things you don't feel comfortable with.

On the other hand, maybe your parents are a little too strict sometimes. If a rule is really bugging you, it's okay to question it. But be smart about it. Come to your parents with a well-thought-out plan of why they should extend a privilege. It's also a good idea to ask for a very small increment of freedom instead of the whole tamale. Parents feel more comfortable granting small exceptions rather than big ones.

For example, maybe your parents want you home from a party by 10 P.M. on a Saturday night; you want to stay out until 11:00. So compromise, and ask to stay out until 10:30. Then, if your parents say yes, don't abuse the privilege. Be home at 10:30 sharp, or really impress your parents and show up ten minutes early. This way, you earn your parents' trust. They see that you're able to handle new freedom responsibly, which will give them incentive to grant you even more privileges in the future.

out of step

Q. My parents have been divorced for a few years and by now I'm pretty used to the arrangement. I spend half the time with my mom, half with my dad.

My mom has been seeing this man for a while and last week she came home and announced that they were engaged. They're planning on getting married in the summer and want me to be the flower girl. I acted all happy, but inside I wanted to cry. The guy my mom is seeing is nice enough and we get along well, but I don't want him living with us. We're fine on our own, and he's just going to wreck our lives, I know it! What can I do to stop my mom from doing this?

Rosa, 12

A. If your mom's mind is made up, there's nothing you can do to stop her from getting married. And while you're hurting now, you won't always feel this way. You just need some time to adjust to the new situation.

Right now, all you can see are the negatives. But keep your eyes open to the positives, too. You say this man is nice and that the two of you get along. That's great! Maybe you'll even come to love him like a dad one day. Think about your mom, too. She's probably been a lot happier since she's hooked up with this man. That's something positive, too.

Also sit down and talk to your mom. It's okay to tell her your feelings because they're completely normal. And you'll feel better once you express yourself. This will give your mom the opportunity to reassure you how much she loves you. Because no matter how many changes your family is going through, that's one thing that will never change.

mortified by mom

Q. My mom wears the weirdest stuff. Sometimes I swear she looks like a bag lady even though she's skinny and could look like a fashion model. She's also got this big, booming voice. When she drops me off at school or when kids see me at the mall with her, sometimes I'm so embarrassed I want to disappear.

I've told her how I feel, and have even given her wardrobe hints, but she just laughs about it. She's not taking me seriously, but *I'm serious*. I know it's

? only time before all the kids at school are going to make fun of me because of her. Help me, please!!!!!!

DeShawn, 13

A. Whoa, there. Don't you think you're being a little hard on your mom? Could it be you're *exaggerating* a bit?

It's okay to do that as long as in your mind you know the difference between fact and fiction. Maybe your mom doesn't dress in Armani, but that doesn't make her a bag lady. But if you keep telling yourself she looks like one, of course you're going to feel embarrassed to be around her. So don't stretch the truth. Even to yourself.

As for others making fun of you, that's probably not gonna happen. Know why? All the kids at school are way too busy stressing over how their *own* parents look and act to even think twice about yours! That's because almost every teen on earth goes through an I-can't-believe-those-dorks-are-my-parents phase. It's in the hormones. Or in the water. Or something.

Anyway, give your mom—and yourself—a break, and stop picking on her. The less you focus on the way she dresses and talks, the less it will bug you in the first place.

P.S. Since she's already dismissed your attempts to change her, it's probably not going to work anyway.

devastated by divorce

Q. My parents just told me that they're getting a divorce. I can't believe it. I'm also feeling really guilty. They say that it has nothing to do with me, but I don't believe it. I scream at them sometimes and can be really moody. Once I even told them I wanted to live somewhere else.

Do you think that maybe I caused the divorce—like my dad, who's moving out, got sick of living with me?

Rachel, 12

A. No way. Don't even go there. The reason your parents are divorcing has nothing to do with you and everything to do with them. Maybe they've fallen out of love. Or are fighting too much. Or can't see eye to eye on the important issues. Whatever the reason, it's not your fault. Dealing with your parents' divorce is tough enough without you trying to shoulder the blame. So don't. Not even for one second.

cinderella story

Q. I have two sisters close to me in age. For some reason, my mom makes me do all the work. I take care of the dog, plus I have to set the table and clear the dishes each

A. Maybe you're doing more than your two sisters, but maybe not. Maybe it only feels that way. Write down all of your weekly responsibilities. Once it's staring back at you in black and white, you may discover that the workload is more equal than you think. In that case, you don't have to feel like Cinderella anymore!

However, if the workload *is* lopsided, it's time to have a chat with your mom. Give her the list and tell her (in a nice way, of course) that you'd like the household chores to be more evenly distributed. Maybe your mom didn't realize you were doing more than anyone else. Or maybe she'll realize that she's gone too easy on your sisters and has allowed them to slide out of their duties.

too much yelling

Q. When my parents get mad at me, it's really scary. They yell at me and tell me I'm no good. I try to do things right, but sometimes I flub up. That's when I get into trouble. I hate being screamed at and don't know what to do. Can you help?

Megan, 12

A. Please know that it's not okay that your parents yell at you and tell you that you're no good. They themselves probably know this is wrong and want to stop. But sometimes people can't quit certain behaviors even when they know they should.

Your parents need help. And so do you. The way to get it is to tell another adult about what's going on at home. This could be a teacher, a school counselor, a coach, an older friend, or another relative. It doesn't matter who it is as long as you trust that person. This adult will be in a position to get involved if needed and try to get your parents, and you, too, into counseling or whatever else it will take to stop them from being verbally abusive. Because that's what they're being.

Be brave. Be strong. And talk to someone today.

living with the cia

Q. My parents are the biggest snoops. My mom barges into my room without knocking, and once I even caught her reading my journal. My dad's always grilling

me about who I'm hanging out with and what I do.
Don't they understand I need space to be myself?
What can I do?

Destiny, 12

A. Your parents aren't respecting your privacy. But think about this. They're used to your being a kid. When you were younger, you didn't mind if they came into your room—you probably wanted them to. And anything you wrote was an open book because you didn't have any big secrets yet, right?

Tell them how important your privacy has become to you and ask that they please respect it. It also wouldn't hurt to get a diary with a lock...just in case.

As for all the questions your dad asks, he's probably not really grilling you or expecting long, detailed answers. He just wants to know in general how you're doing. So give him the condensed version. See if that will satisfy him, and you, too.

Chapter 9:

School
Rules

Y ou're already juggling friends, family, and a gazillion activities. Then there's this little thing called school you've got to spend three-fourths of your day in! And now that you're getting older, the work is getting a lot harder. Plus, there's pressure to do better than ever before.

When you screw up, boy, do you feel stupid. But when you do well, you rule!

Some classes will be easier than others. Some years you'll get better grades than others. But if ever you hit a serious academic pothole in the road, you don't have to continue on alone.

pet project

Q. I'm really good in English, and this year have become the teacher's pet. She's always using me as an example of what to do. The problem is, some of the other kids in the class are starting to resent it. They call me stuff like "egghead" and "butt kisser." I'm not at all. I just love school and work hard. What can I do?

Christina, 13

A. Boy, does that stink when others get down on you for being smart. The kids who tease you are probably just jealous, but still, for sure, it hurts.

It's worth a shot to talk to your teacher. Tell her what's going on. Maybe once she quits being so obvious that you are her favorite, everyone will back off. Or maybe your teacher will have some good suggestions of her own about how you can handle the situation.

Whatever you do, never stop letting your smarts shine. Your brains will pay off again and again, so don't let a few bad apples intimidate you into ever playing dumb.

sudden slump

Q. I'm a pretty good student, but lately I'm having trouble concentrating in class. I get sleepy a lot, and can't focus on what my teacher is saying. The other day my bio teacher asked me a question and I didn't even know what he was talking about! He had to repeat it, twice. I was so embarrassed. Plus, I could tell he was really disappointed in me. Why can't I concentrate anymore?

Patricia, 12

A. A couple of things may be going on. First of all, your eating habits may be fueling your funk. What, for example, are you eating for breakfast? If you're filling up on foods loaded with sugar, you won't be able to focus well in class. Sugar gives you an immediate boost, but a half hour or so later, you feel more tired than you did to start with. So try sticking to the healthy stuff, such as oatmeal, whole wheat toast, fruit, eggs, unsweetened cereal, or a bagel and cream cheese.

Lunch may be the same story. If you push away your turkey sandwich and go for only cookies, your energy level is bound to stall out come one o'clock in the afternoon.

Also, how much water are you drinking? A lot of people walk around dehydrated all day because they don't drink enough. All of us need at least six to eight glasses a day. If you're dehydrated, you'll feel fuzzy-headed and weak. So take a trip to the water fountain before class begins. Or keep a water bottle on your desk, if it's okay with your teacher.

Last but not least, make sure you get enough sleep at night. You need about nine or ten hours a night. Any less, and you're gonna feel sleepy during the day.

test of her nerves

Q. Here's my problem. I study and study and study, and then when it comes time to take the test, I blow it. I make stupid mistakes and get so nervous that it's hard to think. What can I do to ever get over this?

Ami, 13

A. Sounds like you need to slow down a little. You could be rushing, which explains all the careless mistakes. So make sure you read each question carefully and take your time answering.

As for your nerves, try this: At home the night before a test, close your eyes and imagine that you're in the classroom taking the test. "See" yourself slowly but surely marking down the right answers. Then "see" yourself getting the paper back with 100 percent on it. What this does is plant the suggestion in your mind that you'll ace the test. You walk into the classroom with an extra dose of confidence that will help you relax.

the college trap

Q. I'm only in eighth grade, but my parents are already obsessed with what college I'll get into. They're on me to get really good grades because they want me to go to a top school like they did. So if I even get an A-, they freak. I work hard and do my best, but I can't take the pressure. So what if I get a B now and then? I'm sure some college will take me. What can I do to get my parents to stop putting so much pressure on me?

Lucy, 14

A. Getting into a good college is important, but not that important! On the other hand, it's not too hard to see why your parents are so obsessed. All you hear about these days is how competitive it is to get into college. Teachers talk about it. So do the counselors. And the media. So it's no wonder parents start wigging out!

You need to sit down with your parents and tell them how you're feeling. They might not realize how hard they're pushing you. Or maybe they've thought they had to or you wouldn't work hard. Once they know how you feel, they might let up on you. Your parents obviously care about you or they wouldn't want so much for you. Hopefully they'll care enough to change.

passing phase

Q. Two of my best friends are in math class with me and it's getting me into a lot of trouble. Sometimes we talk and giggle and pass notes. Then our teacher gets really mad. Once she even sent us to the principal's office. I want to start over and stop getting into trouble. But I'm not sure my teacher will give me a chance. What can I do to prove it to her that I'm a good student?

Angela, 12

A. Apologize and tell her that from now on, she's going to see a new, improved you. Also ask her if you could move away from your friends because the farther away they are, the less you'll be tempted to chat.

Next, have a little powwow with your pals and tell them no more note-passing. If one tries to wing one your way anyway, ignore it. And don't write one yourself even if you're bursting with news you feel just can't wait.

It may take a few weeks. But if you keep up the good behavior, your teacher's opinion of you is bound to change.

Chapter 10:

You're **Looking Good,** Girl

Used to be that you were out the door in one minute flat. All you had to do was throw some water on your face and drag a comb through your hair and you were ready.

But lately, you've slowed down. In between applying your makeup, fixing your hair, and doing your nails, it can take you hours to leave the house.

But even though your beauty routine's gotten more complicated, do your best to keep it simple.

brow beauty

> **Q.** My eyebrows are so gross. They're black and bushy and meet in the middle. All my friends pluck theirs, and I want to start, too. Problem is, I have no idea how to do it. I'm also worried it will hurt. Will it?
>
> Stephanie, 13

A. A little. But you can make it as painless as possible by tweezing after you take a shower or a bath. The warm water will open up your skin's pores and make the hairs slide out easier. Or else you can place a warm washcloth over your eyes to soften the skin.

It also helps to use tweezers that have slightly rounded tips. Pointy ones can stab your skin. Flat ones have such a hard time grabbing the hair that sometimes you end up grabbing your skin as well. Ouch!

As for shaping your eyebrows, first pluck all the hairs in between. Your brows should start at the inner corners of your eyes; make sure you don't pluck farther in.

Next, thin out each brow, plucking one hair at a time from underneath, not on top of the brow. Move from the inner corner to the outer corner of each eye. The brow should start out thick and get thinner as it extends over your eye. And don't let the front of the brow be lower than the end or you'll look like you're frowning.

Once you get the shape you want, use an old tooth-brush to brush your brows up. You can also spritz hair spray on the toothbrush to help your brows stay in place.

The biggest mistake girls make when plucking is that they don't know when to stop and end up with too-skinny brows. So don't get carried away. Remember, you can always pluck more tomorrow if you still think your brows look too bushy.

sink your teeth into this

A. Most nail nibblers are nervous sorts. When you get stressed, you get munching. So one solution is to find another way to handle tension. Taking a walk, writing down your feelings in your journal, screaming into a pillow, or jumping up and down are all good stress-busters. So give them a shot and see if they save your nails.

Another idea is to paint your nails (or what's left of them) the brightest color you can find, like electric blue. You probably bite your nails without even thinking. The bright color will help call attention to your nails—and to the fact that you're about to bite them. Hopefully you can then catch yourself in the act and stop before you start.

One more trick: When the urge to chew your nails strikes, chomp on a piece of gum instead. Over time, you'll start reaching for the gum automatically.

Q. I've thought a lot about it and I want to start shaving my legs. Most of my friends have already been doing it for a while. But how do I shave without cutting myself and looking like I've just walked off the set of some slasher film? Can you give me any pointers?

Kaylee, 12

A. You don't have to be a cutup when it comes to shaving your legs. Just follow these safe and sensible tips:

✳ Use a plastic disposable razor.

✳ Shave your legs during your bath or shower or immediately afterward because the water will soften the hairs. Also, lather up with soap or shaving cream, because they will help the razor glide smoothly over your skin.

✳ Rinse out your razor frequently so it doesn't get clogged with hair and soap.

✳ Take your time. Use special care around your knees and shins because the bones make it difficult for a razor to get around those areas.

✳ After shaving, put on some lotion so your legs don't become dry or irritated. And if you did get a nick, don't freak. Just put pressure on it with your finger or a tissue and hold it for a couple of minutes.

makeup madness

> **Q.** Some of the girls at school wear tons of makeup, like mascara, eyeliner, and foundation. I don't think it looks that good, but some of my friends do. And I've heard guys say it looks cool. I don't wear any makeup. But if I did, maybe I'd look better. Do most girls look better with a lot of makeup on or just being themselves?
>
> Donatella, 13

A. The answer lies somewhere in between. Most girls look best with just a tad of makeup.

Girls who pile it on can look harsh and way too old for their age. Plus, it takes up so much time putting it on and reapplying it all day long.

Usually guys aren't into the made-up look, either. They prefer the more natural look.

If you're ready to experiment with cosmetics, start with a lip gloss or light lipstick. Then add some clear mascara to make your eyes stand out. The wet coating will make your lashes look longer and bring out your eyes.

Finally, brush on a little blush. Go for a powder blush because it's the easiest to glide over your cheeks. As for colors, choose something neutral, like golden brown or tan.

And remember, even if you *do* wear a little makeup, you're still "yourself." A little blush and mascara won't change that.

your biggest beauty asset

Q. What do you think it takes to make a girl pretty? I say it's her complexion. My friend, however, thinks it's a girl's hair. She's always wanted thick, blond hair (her hair is thin and brown) and says that if her hair were different, it would change her life. What do you think?

Nora, 13

A. It's not a girl's hair or skin or features or figure that makes her pretty. Hate to go completely corny on you, but it's her attitude. If she's kind. Considerate. Good to others—as well as herself. Because girls like this have an inner beauty that shows on the outside.

So don't fret about your skin. And tell your friend not to worry so about her hair. You both probably already have what it takes to be beautiful. Look inside to be sure.

Conclusion

Hopefully throughout this book you've learned some advice that you can use to solve a problem in your life—or to help a friend.

It's not always easy growing up, but it can be exciting, too. If you try to focus on the positive stuff, the negative stuff won't seem so bad.

And no matter what you do, always be true to yourself. Deep down, you know what's right for you.